NIGHTY NIGHT, NOAH

An Ark Alphabet

by

Molly Schaar Idle

Abingdon Press

Nashville

Nighty Night, Noah

978-0-687-64691-3

08 09 10 11 12 13 14 15 16 17—10 9 8 7 6 5 4 3 2 1

Printed in China

To my Two
John and Tom

For 40 Days and 40 Nights rain fell upon the ark,
Now all aboard catch 40 winks as daylight turns to dark.

Noah tucks them, two by two, into their beds with care
To see that each from A to Z will sleep in cozy pairs.

Alligators brush their teeth
till each is pearly white.

Bears each need a big bear hug
to see them through the night.

Camels need *another* drink   before they go to bed . . .

Doves fall asleep with feathered pillows
'neath their peaceful heads.

Elephants remember
to say "thank you" in their prayers
For friends and food — like peanuts . . .
All the blessings that are theirs.

F G

Flamingos and Giraffes
need extra blankets for, you see,

One needs covers for their necks — the other for their knees!

Hippopotami are heavy sleepers
when they hit the sack!

Ibises, their earmuffed neighbors,
are insomniacs.

Jackrabbits and **K**angaroos are jumping on their beds.

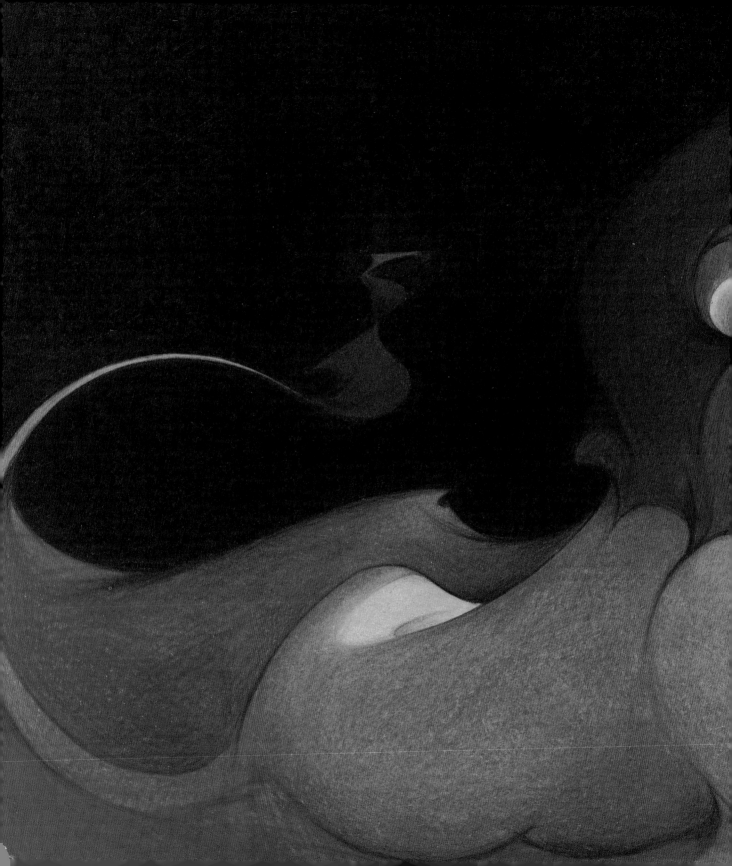

Lions roar in protest —
"One more story must be
read!"

Mice are barely stirring as the ark rocks in the drink.

Night owls are nocturnal. They won't sleep a single wink.

O P

Ostriches and **P**ossums
are the oddest sleepers found.

One pair dozes upside down —
the other underground!

Quails' sleepy heads bob up and down —
each with a plume adorned.

Rhinoceros wear sleeping caps
upon their heads and horns.

Sheep count themselves to fall asleep
as they lie in the moonlight.

Tortoises, tucked in their shells,
can be sure they will sleep tight.

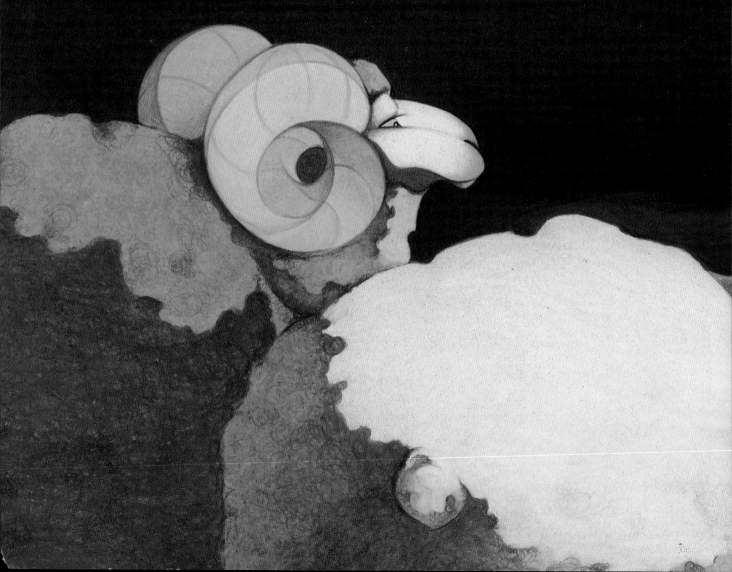

Underwater —
animals are snoozing in the deep.

Violet Fish and Whales
'neath the waves are fast asleep.

X - Ray Fish —
like nightlights —
can illuminate the dark
For all the creatures in the ocean
underneath the ark.

Yaks stop yakking and start yawning —
rocked to sleep upon the seas.

Nighty Night now, Noah,
it is time to catch some
Zzzzzzzzz.

"Now I lay me down to sleep,
I pray the Lord my soul to keep . . ."